THE WEAPONS ENCYCLOPÆDIA
TANK AIRCRAFT AFV SHIP ARTILLERY VEHICLES SECRET WEAPON

TWE-036 ENG

POLISH 7TP LIGHT TANK

THE WEAPONS ENCYCLOPAEDIA

EDITORIAL STAFF
Luca Cristini, Paolo Crippa.

ACADEMIC STAFF
Enrico Acerbi, Massimiliano Afiero, Aldo Antonicelli, Ruggero Calò, Luigi Carretta, Flavio Chistè, Anna Cristini, Carlo Cucut, Salvo Fagone, Enrico Finazzer, Arturo Giusti, Björn Huber, Andrea Lombardi, Aymeric Lopez, Marco Lucchetti, Gabriele Malavoglia, Luigi Manes, Giovanni Maressi, Francesco Mattesini, Daniele Notaro, Péter Mujzer, Federico Peirani, Alberto Peruffo, Maurizio Raggi, Andrea Alberto Tallillo, Antonio Tallillo, Roberto Vela, Massimo Zorza.

PUBLISHED BY
Luca Cristini Editore (Soldiershop), via Orio, 35/4 - 24050 Zanica (BG) ITALY.

DISTRIBUTION BY
Soldiershop - www.soldiershop.com, Amazon, Ingram Spark, Berliner Zinnfigurem (D), LaFeltrinelli, Mondadori, Libera Editorial (Spain), Google book (eBook), Kobo, (eBoook), Apple Book (eBook).

PUBLISHING'S NOTES
None of unpublished images or text of our book may be reproduced in any format without the expressed written permission of Luca Cristini Editore (already Soldiershop.com) when not indicate as marked with license creative commons 3.0 or 4.0. Luca Cristini Editore has made every reasonable effort to locate, contact and acknowledge rights holders and to correctly apply terms and conditions to Content. Every effort has been made to trace the copyright of all the photographs. If there are unintentional omissions, please contact the publisher in writing at: info@soldiershop.com, who will correct all subsequent editions.

LICENSES COMMONS
This book may utilize part of material marked with license creative commons 3.0 or 4.0 (CC BY 4.0), (CC BY-ND 4.0), (CC BY-SA 4.0) or (CC0 1.0). We give appropriate attribution credit and indicate if change were made in the acknowledgments field. Our WTW books series utilize only fonts licensed under the SIL Open Font License or other free use license.

CONTRIBUTORS OF THIS VOLUME & ACKNOWLEDGEMENTS
We would like to thank the main contributors to this issue: The profiles of the floats are all by the author. The colouring of the photos is by Anna Cristini. Special thanks to national and/or private institutions such as: Army General Staff, State Archives, Bundesarchiv, Nara, Library of Congress, Wikipedia, USAF, Signal magazine, War Chronicles, War Front, IWM, Australian War Museum, etc. A P.Crippa, A.Lopez, Péter Mujzer, L.Manes, C.Cucut, Tallillo archives. Model Victoria (www.modelvictoria.it) etc. for making available pictures or anything else from their archives. Special thanks to all modellers, their clubs and modelling companies for the courtesy use of their images. As far as possible we will always include the names of the authors. Please let us know in case you have not been able to locate them.

For a complete list of Soldiershop titles, or for every information please contact us on our website: www.soldiershop.com or www.cristinieditore.com. E-mail: info@soldiershop.com. Keep up to date on Facebook https://www.facebook.com/soldiershop.publishing

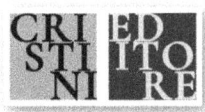

Title: **POLISH 7TP LIGHT TANK** Code.: **TWE-036 EN**
Series by L. S. Cristini
ISBN code: 979-12-5589-2182 First edition March 2025
THE WEAPONS ENCYCLOPAEDIA (SOLDIERSHOP) is a trademark of Luca Cristini Editore

THE WEAPONS ENCYCLOPÆDIA
TANK AIRCRAFT AFV SHIP ARTILLERY VEHICLES SECRET WEAPON

POLISH 7TP LIGHT TANK

FROM THE BRITISH VICKERS MK. E TO THE NATIONAL VERSION

LUCA STEFANO CRISTINI

BOOK SERIES FOR MODELLERS & COLLECTORS

CONTENTS

Introduction .... Pag. 5
- From the British Mk. E Vickers to the Polish 7TP .... Pag. 5
- History and development of the Polish light tank .... Pag. 9
- The first Polish improvements .... Pag. 11
- Towards the final 7TP tank .... Pag. 13

Technical features .... Pag. 21

Versions of the vehicle .... Pag. 23
- Vickers'0 variants A and B .... Pag. 25
- The G7P artillery tractor .... Pag. 28
- Other variants .... Pag. 36

Operational use .... Pag. 41
- Pre-war operations .... Pag. 41
- The 1939 campaign .... Pag. 47

Camouflage and markings .... Pag. 55

Other users and data sheet .... Pag. 57

Periscope Gundlach .... Pag. 59

Bibliography .... Pag. 70

▲ The only known reconstruction of a Polish 7TP using parts from several examples, then assembled together and exhibited at the Muzeum Polskiej Techniki Wojskowej in 2015. Wiki cc3.

INTRODUCTION

■ FROM THE BRITISH MK. E VICKERS TO THE POLISH 7TP

The 7TP was a light tank designed and produced in Poland, used mainly during the early stages of World War II to counter the German invasion. Recall that in the 1930s, Poland had a limited armored force, consisting exclusively of light tanks, which until then had been considered adequate. However, growing tensions with Germany prompted the Polish military leadership to accelerate the mechanization of the army.

As a result of this, in 1931, Poland ordered 50 Vickers Mk. E six-ton tanks from the United Kingdom, 7-ton light vehicles that, while not particularly popular with the British Army, were commercially successful abroad and were sold by Vickers-Armstrong to various countries, often accompanied by a manufacturing license.

Between 1932 and 1933, Poland received the first 16 double-turret tanks (Model A) and 22 single-turret models (Model B), while the remaining 12 remained in the UK as part of the license payment and later joined the others in dismounted form. The double turret tanks were armed with two machine gunsCkm wz.. 25 Hotchkiss 7.92 mm, while the single turret ones mounted a 47 mm gun and a Browning wz. 30 of 7.92 mm.

After the usual series of tests, PZI's engineering department, at the Army's request, developed a program called VAU-33 (Vickers-Armstrong-Ursus 33), with the goal of creating from scratch single- or double-turret tanks from the very design of the Vickers Mk. E Model A.

The two versions were familiarly referred to by Polish soldiers as "dw" and "jw," abbreviations of the Polish words "dwuwieżowy" (double turret) and "jednowieżowy" (single turret), although this form was never officially used by Polish sources or the army. In the early years the standard model was the double turret one, but both this and the single turret one were since then commonly referred to by the name 7TP, thus completing this strange transition.

▲ A British Vickers Mk E light tank, ancestor of the entire creation of the Polish 7TP series tanks.

In essence, the 7TP represented the Polish evolution of the British tank. The differences from the original model are that the 7TP introduced several improvements, including a more powerful and reliable diesel engine, a 37 mm anti-tank gun, thicker front armor (17 mm instead of 13 mm), a modified ventilation system, the national periscope *Gundlach*, and the installation of a radio. Between 1935 and the beginning of the war, some 132 examples were built in addition to the 50 "British" ones, as well as four prototypes made of iron. The name "7TP" stood for "7 tons, Polish," although the actual weight of the tank increased to 9 tons over the initial prototype.

Although the 7TP is often considered the world's first production diesel tank, this record actually belongs to the Japanese Type 89B I-Go Otsu, equipped with a diesel engine as early as 1934. Another contender in that race was the Type 95 Ha-Go, also mass-produced since 1935 and considered the first tank specifically designed with a diesel engine.

Like the Vickers Mark E, the 7TP was initially produced in two versions: a double turret version, armed with two machine guns Ckm wz.30, and a single turret version, equipped with a gun. Bofors 37 mm wz.37 However, during testing it emerged that the double turret variant was now obsolete and lacking in firepower, leading to its gradual replacement by the single turret model. Before the outbreak of World War II, most of the double-turret tanks were permanently converted to the single-turret version, leaving only 24 double-turret units in service, compared with about 108 of the other type.

In 1938, the Państwowe Zakłady Inżynierii also developed 13 prototypes of an improved and better armored version of the 7TP, called the 9TP. Although this model never went into mass production, the prototypes were still employed during the desperate defense of Warsaw in September 1939.

▲ The Polish light tank, here in the British version with two turrets, had a crew of three, with the commander and secondary gunner located in the two turrets. The pilot was seated low down on the right side of the hull.

◀ 1932: Polish Vickers tanks under construction in England. The Polish army expressly requested that no armament be supplied. (AP)

▲ The interior of the PZI production facilities of the 7TP tank. Polish archives (AP). Above right: a Vickers of the type with two turrets during testing (AP). Above left: parade of Polish Vickers Mk. E tanks. In the background, right: the Vickers prototype equipped and tested with radio equipment.

POLISH 7TP LIGHT TANK

VICKERS MK. E TWO-TURRET LIGHT TANK, POLAND 1933

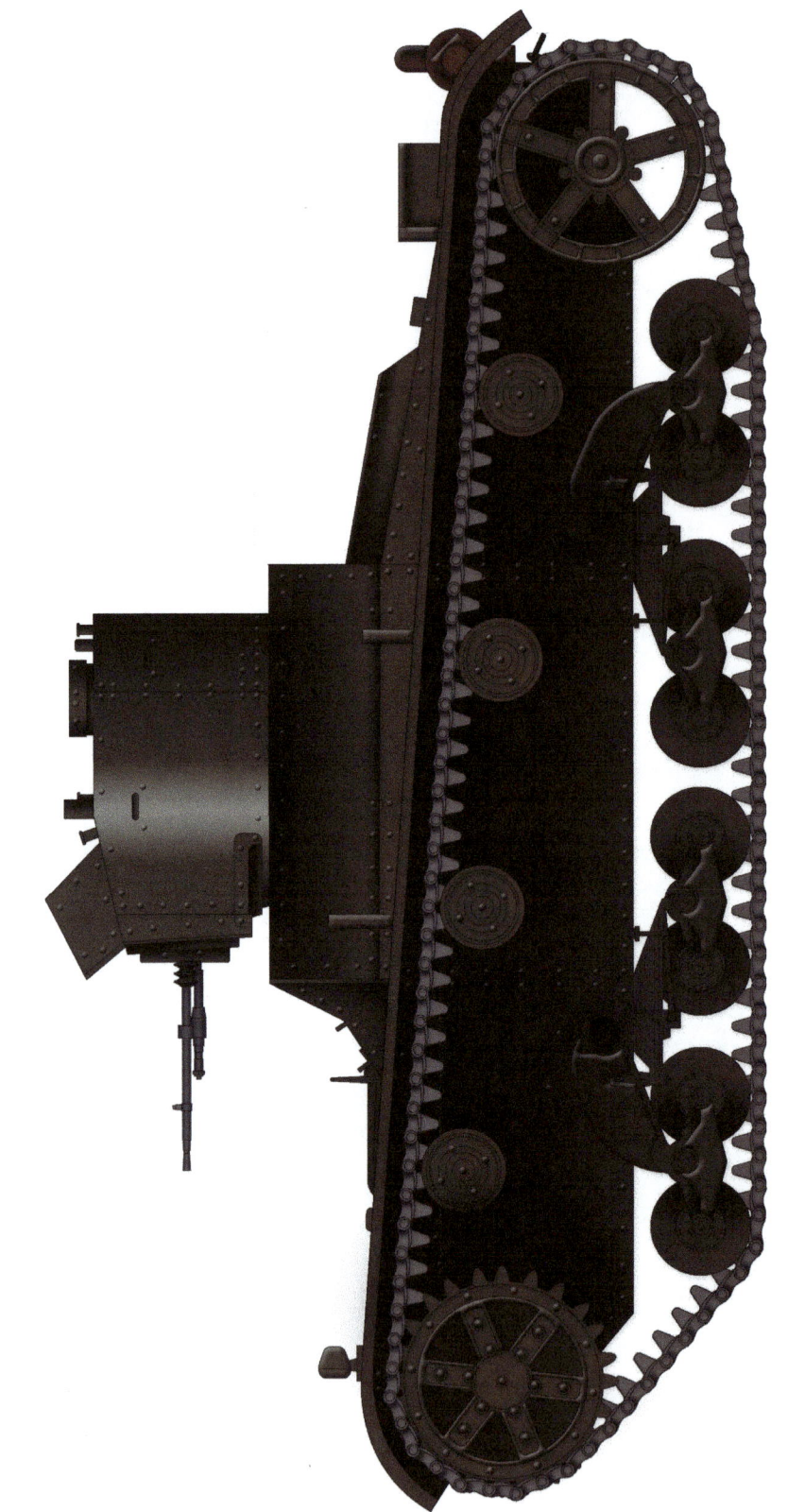

▲ Polish Army Vickers Mark E light tank with two 7.92 mm Hotchkiss wz.25 air-cooled machine guns. Poland 1933.

HISTORY AND DEVELOPMENT OF THE POLISH LIGHT TANK

In the mid-1920s it became clear that the Polish Army needed modern tanks to replace the aging Renault FTs dating back to World War I that represented their armored force at the time. However, local engineers of the time did not have sufficient know-how to develop such designs. They therefore opted, as mentioned above, to purchase a license abroad, which would provide a technological base on which to develop independent designs. In parallel, a design competition was held among Polish engineers in April 1926, but the only prototype built in 1928, the WB-10 tank, turned out to be a failure.

Beginning in 1925, the Polish government initiated contacts with the British company Vickers-Armstrongs, one of the few well-known tank manufacturers at the time. On July 31, 1925, the Polish Armaments Committee expressed its intention to purchase 50 Vickers tanks, in particular they had their eye on the Medium Mark II model, which met Polish requirements. However, the British government did not authorize the export of these vehicles. At that time, the Polish Army was interested in 10- to 12-ton tanks, which they always classified as "light" but actually equivalent to British Medium tanks. Toward the end of 1925, Vickers then proposed to Poland the Mark C medium tank, originally developed for Japan, which was reviewed in January 1927. But again no agreement was reached. the same offer was relaunched with an improved version: the Mark D, which, however, continued to be disliked by the Polish authorities, mainly because of insufficient armor In August 1927, the Committee on Armament and Equipment (KSUS) finally approved the purchase of 30 unspecified Vickers tanks. It was an interim choice, made pending a final solution. In short, the negotiations were struggling to get off the ground.

In 1928, Vickers-Armstrongs completed the development of a new 6-ton tank, known as the Mark E (Mk.E), which represented a significant breakthrough in tank design. This vehicle was designed in two variants: the Type A, with twin turrets armed with machine guns, and the Type B, with a single turret equipped with a coaxial gun and machine gun, an innovative configuration for the time. The first sketches of the Mark E were shown to the Polish delegation in February 1928, which, however, waited until 1930, Poland before returning to consider the new option revived by Vickers.

▲ The mammoth, slow and expensive Polish supertanker WB-10, here in a very rare picture of it. It turned out to be a complete failure and the Poles preferred to turn abroad.

VICKERS MK. E TWO-TURRET LIGHT TANK, POLAND 1933

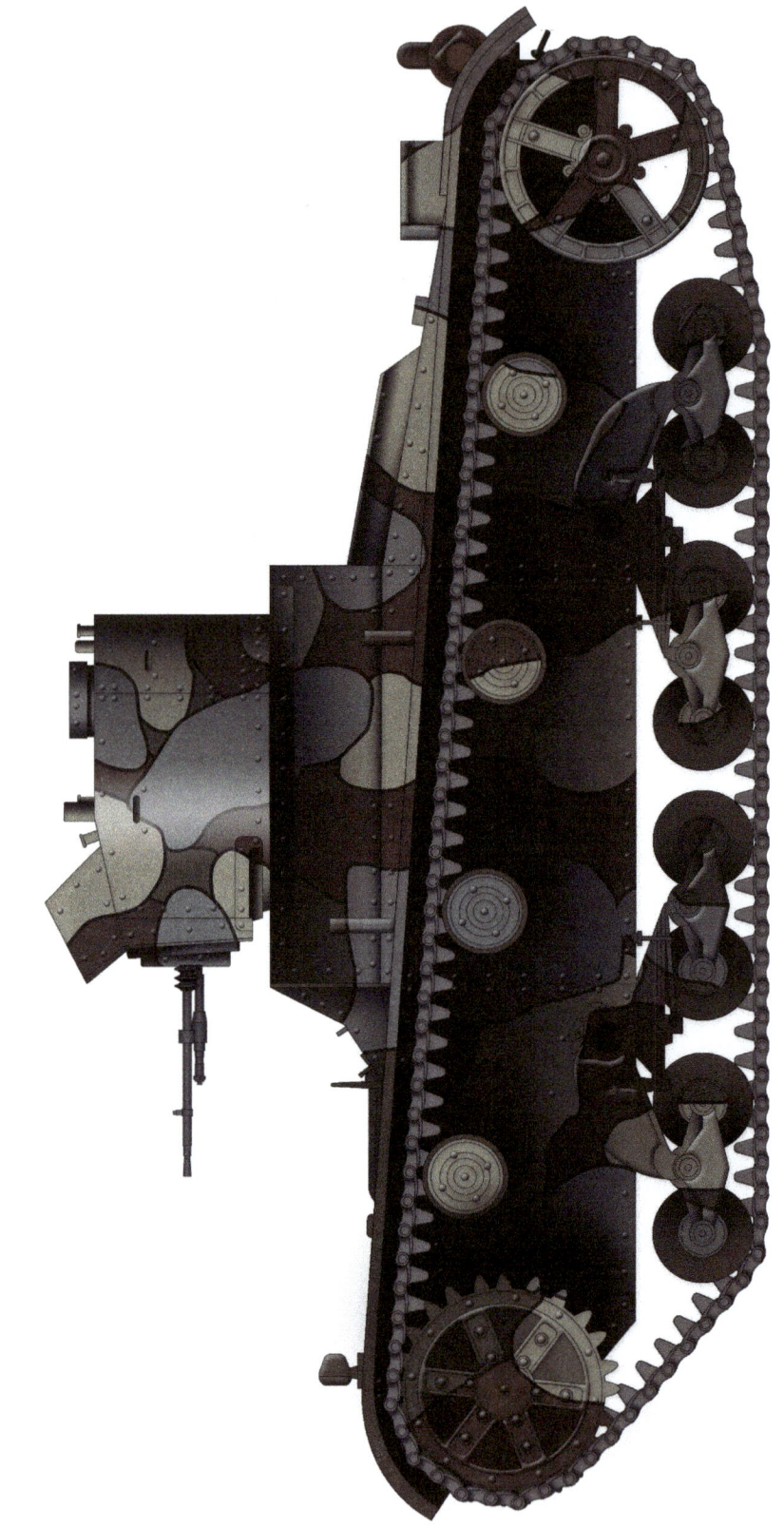

▲ Polish Army Vickers Mark E light tank with two 7.92 mm Hotchkiss wz.25 air-cooled machine guns. Shown here in the rich camouflage version. Poland 1933.

The first Mark E was tested in Poland in September 1930, demonstrating good performance despite some problems, such as engine overheating and thin armor. after a brief interest in a U.S. model Poland negotiated the purchase of 38 Mk.E Type A tanks, along with spare parts and a production license, becoming at the same time Vickers' largest customer. The initial cost per tank was 3,800 pounds, which following negotiation dropped to about 3,100 pounds due to problems found in the armor. Despite some limitations, Vickers tanks were still considered an important step toward modernizing the Polish Army.
Huge economic problems allowed Poland to produce only just under 150 light tanks before the outbreak of World War II.

THE FIRST POLISH IMPROVEMENTS

The first dozen tanks ordered from Poland were supposed to be delivered between March and July 1932, but delivery slipped to early 1933. All the first vehicles to arrive belonged to the double turret variant (Type A). After the first tests, the Poles immediately introduced a number of significant modifications. Initially, a new oil cooler was installed, protected by an armored cover. Next, large and highly visible side vents were added behind the battle compartment, similar to grates, a key improvement for engine cooling. This feature, unique in Polish Vickers tanks, was implemented between the winter of 1934 and the spring of 1935.

These modifications, along with other minor upgrades, were designed by Vickers but made in Poland, at the workshops of the 3rd Armored Battalion and the factories PZInż. , at Vickers' own expense. All tanks were officially accepted by the Polish Army by August 1934, after completion of modifications and a test over a 1,000-km route conducted with two examples. Between 1934 and 1935, 22 tanks were suitably converted to the standard Type B, equipped with a single turret.

▲ Off-road evaluation test of the Polish Vickers Mk E in 1933 (the vehicle appears unarmoured). Vickers tanks in a two-turret configuration used a simple cylindrical shape with a projection for the main armour.

VICKERS MK. E LIGHT TANK WITH SINGLE TURRET, POLAND 1934

▲ Polish Army Vickers Mark E light tank with single turret and 4.7 cm Vickers short-barreled gun. Shown here in the later rich camouflage version. Poland 1934.

Polish tanks were distinguished from all other Vickers produced and exported by the British, mainly by their large side air intakes, which channeled air to the air-cooled engine. After 1935, the Polish tanks received further improvements, including rear toolboxes placed on the fenders, which gave them a silhouette similar to the future 7TP. The double-turreted tanks were recognisable by the large magazine covers of the 13.2 mm Hotchkiss machine guns, which remained in use despite the withdrawal of these weapons from service.

■ TOWARD THE ULTIMATE 7TP TANK

Because of the many shortcomings and problems that emerged during use and testing, it was decided not to produce any more Vickers tanks. However, in late 1932, Poland initiated an improvement project, initially designated VAU-33 (Vickers-Armstrong-Ursus 1933) and later renamed 7TP (7-ton, Polish). The most significant upgrade was the adoption of a more powerful and reliable water-cooled Diesel engine, which required a raised engine compartment, altering the outline of the tank. Suspension and armor were also reinforced and, finally, a good 37 mm anti-tank gun was installed. The resulting 7TP is considered the most successful tank in the Vickers E. The turrets removed from the twin-turret Vickers were reused in the first series of 7TP, which retained this duality: single or twin. Another interesting development was the C7P artillery tractor.

Throughout 1936 efforts were made to modernize the Vickers to the 7TP standard. One example, number 1359, was equipped with a PZInż.235 diesel engine (Saurer VBLDb), improved transmission, reinforced suspension, and thicker armor plates. This vehicle, named the V7TP, demonstrated superior performance, but the project was abandoned in December 1936 due to high conversion costs, estimated at nearly 68,000 złoty per unit, a figure too high. The fate of the converted tank remains uncertain to this day.

▲ One of the first tests of the newcomer: the 7TP light tank in 1936.

VICKERS MK. E TWO-TURRET LIGHT TANK WITH 13.2 MM GUN, POLAND 1934

▲ Polish Vickers Mark E light tank with a 13.2 mm heavy machine gun positioned in the right turret and engine modification. In this version one can clearly see the engine cooling grates placed approximately in the middle of the vehicle.

In 1937, it was proposed to install the anti-tank gun Bofors 37 mm wz.37 on the Vickers, which was even better performing than the 7TP turret. However, lack of funds and wear and tear on the vehicles, now intended primarily for training, scuppered the project. Reinforcement of the armor with stronger plates was also considered, but, due to lack of resources, was never implemented, although it would have significantly improved protection against anti-tank guns.

From the mid-1930s, the development of armored and mechanized troops required increasing numbers of trained officers. Poland, belatedly, ran for cover by organizing schools and specialization courses. Between the two world wars, schools for officers and reserve officers trained about 10,000 officers, non-commissioned officers, and military personnel.

According to a detailed report prepared after the 1939 defeat, the shortcomings of the Polish armored forces were: poor reconnaissance, shortage of armor and artillery, lack of air cover, unreliable communications, insufficient technical and repair personnel, inadequate medical coverage, and lack of all-terrain vehicles. Poland made great efforts to create an armored corps, but its units made the fatal mistake of adopting French doctrine, which prioritized support for infantry and cavalry.

◄ Beautiful picture of the demonstration and performance of the Vickers Mk. E performed in front of a large audience, who came to see the military manoeuvres of the Polish army.

▼ Parade of Vickers Mark E Type B light tanks in marching column during training camp. Polish Archive.

VICKERS MK. E TWO-TURRET LIGHT TANK WITH RADIO SYSTEM, POLAND 1934

▲ Vickers Mark E prototype light tank equipped and tested with antenna and radio equipment. Poland 1934.

VICKERS MK. E LIGHT TANK WITH SINGLE TURRET, POLAND 1934

▲ Polish Army Vickers Mark E light tank with single turret and 4.7 cm Vickers short-barreled gun. Shown here in a camouflage variant and increased silhouette. Poland 1934.

▲ Vickers tanks had their military baptism with participation in the Polish occupation by Czechoslovakia.

▶ A close-up view of the Vickers 4.7 cm short-barreled pistol mount.

▼ The 6-ton Vickers Mk- E was one of the most successful tanks in history.

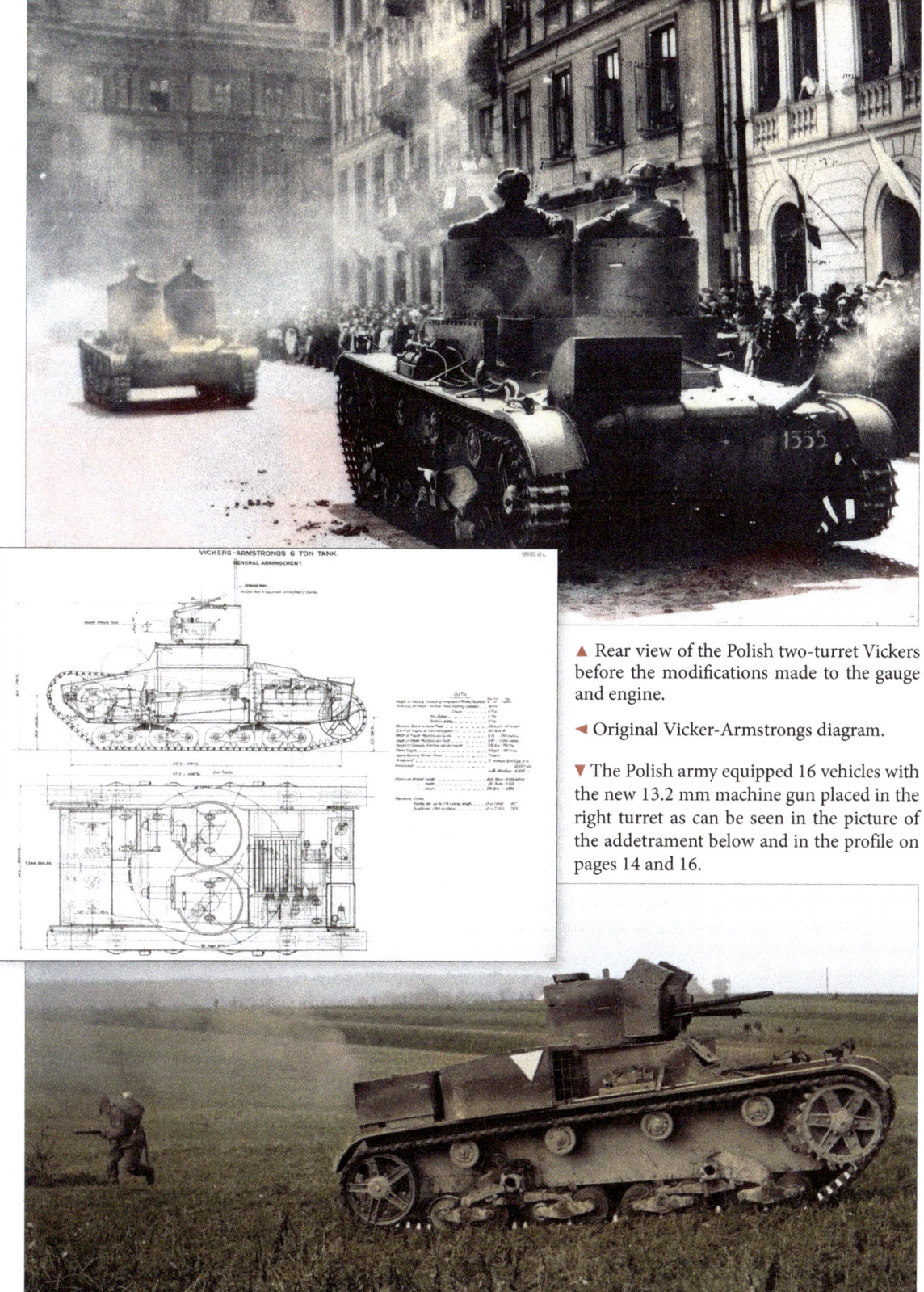

▲ Rear view of the Polish two-turret Vickers before the modifications made to the gauge and engine.

◄ Original Vicker-Armstrongs diagram.

▼ The Polish army equipped 16 vehicles with the new 13.2 mm machine gun placed in the right turret as can be seen in the picture of the addetrament below and in the profile on pages 14 and 16.

7TP LIGHT TANK WITH DOUBLE TURRET, POLAND 1936

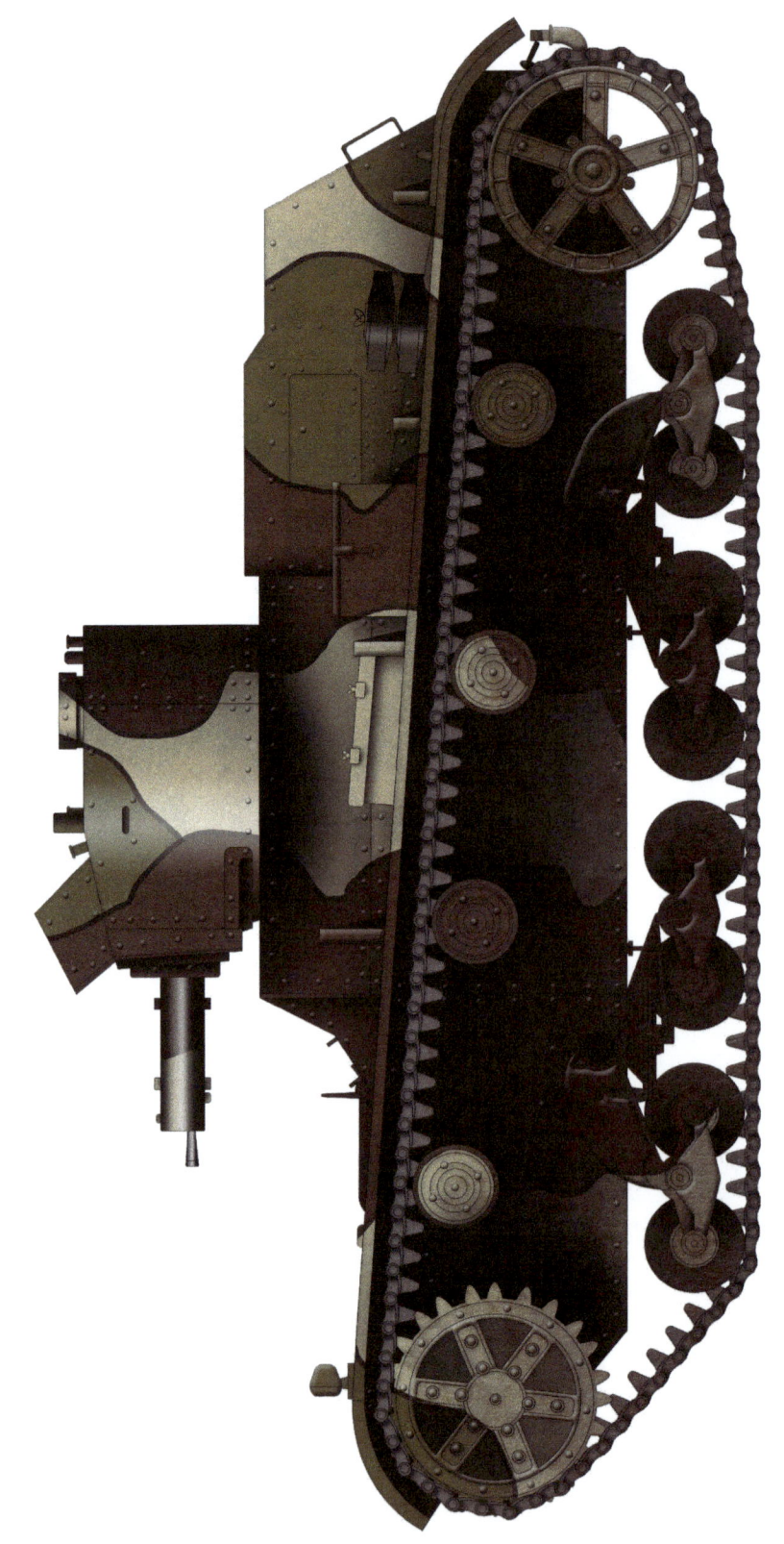

▲ Polish light tank 7TP DW (double turret) 2nd prototype, Poland 1936.

TECHNICAL FEATURES

■ STRUCTURE AND DESIGN

The 7TP tank had a traditional design, divided into three main sections: the front drive, the central compartment or combat chamber, and the engine in the rear. The hull was constructed of laminated armor plates attached to a frame by bolts. The crew consisted of three people. The driver sat in the right front, with a two-door hatch and a simple periscope for a view, but this offered limited visibility, especially in combat. There was then the commander who operated from the turret assisted by an assistant gunner.

■ THE TURRETS

Double Turret: The first version of the 7TP had two small turrets, single-top, each with a top hatch. The commander sat in the right turret, while the gunner occupied the left turret. The first turrets were equipped with 13.2 mm machine guns, used only in Vickers tanksMk.E.

Single Turret: The main version had a conical turret for two people, positioned on the left. The commander, on the right, was responsible for loading the gun and spotting targets, while the gunner, on the left, aimed and fired. The turret was equipped with a forward-opening hatch, a reversible periscope for a 360-degree view and two fixed periscopes. Later for the "Polish" version of the 7TP a new and more modern turret was studied and designed.
The reversible periscope was patented by R. Gundlach and allowed the commander easy all-around observation. The Gundlach periscope acted as a simple rotating periscope for looking forward and sideways, which required turning the head to the side, but thanks to an additional prism extending downward, the commander did not have to turn his head around the periscope to scan the area behind him.

■ ENGINE AND TRANSMISSION

The engine on the first Vickers tanks of both types was an 80-hp Armstrong-Siddeley 4-cylinder. In the final Polish version they switched instead to diesel with a PZInż. 235 (Saurer VGLD) or a 6-cylinder diesel, both water-cooled 6-cylinder diesel engines with an output of 110 hp. VBLDb
The engine was located in the rear compartment, with radiators and side fans. The transmission included a multi-disc dry clutch, a gearbox with 4 forward and 1 reverse gears, and band brakes.
The engine was centrally located in a rear compartment. Two vertical water coolers with fans were located on either side of the engine: air was drawn in through two grilles in the front of a horizontal plate above the engine compartment and exited through two holes in the rear of this plate. In the early series it also came out through the louvers in the rear doors.

■ SUSPENSIONS

The tank used a modified Vickers suspension, with two bogies on each side, each with twin wheels suspended on leaf springs. The suspension was designed to reduce stress on the springs, improving stability.

■ RADIO COMMUNICATIONS

From 1938, some single turret tanks were equipped with a Polish N2/C radio, used mainly by battalion, company, and platoon commanders. The radio had a transmitting antenna up to 6 meters high and a range of 10 km for voice and 25 km for Morse code. Tanks with radios were also equipped with a crew intercom.

ARMAMENT

Armament of the Double Turret: Armed with two 7.92 mm wz.30 machine guns with about 6,000 rounds. From Vickers to Polish models, various machine guns and gun/machine gun pairings were tested over time.

Single turret armament: Armed with a wz.37 mm cannon (Bofors) and a 7.92 mm wz.30 coaxial machine gun. The cannon had 80 rounds, with a rate of fire of 10 rounds per minute. The machine gun had 3960 rounds, carried in 12 boxes. Only four rounds were stowed in the turret, to the right of the cannon; sometimes they also stowed extra ammunition in the rear niche of the turret in tanks without radios. The rest of the ammunition was carried in the hull. The maximum rate of fire was 10 rounds per minute. The guns had a wz.37 CA telescopic sight between the gun and MG, and a wz.37 CA periscope sight on the left side of the roof. The periscope sight was based on the Zeiss TWZ-1.

ARMOUR

The reinforcement made of rolled steel plates varied in thickness depending on the area:
- Hull: Front 17 mm, sides 17 mm to 9 mm, back 9 mm.
- Driver door: 10 mm
- Single turret: Sides and mantle 15 mm, roof 8-10 mm.
- Double turret: sides 13 mm, roof 5 mm.
- Top: 10 mm on the front 5mm on the rest.
- Bottom: 10 mm on the front 5mm on the rest.

CONCLUSIONS

The 7TP tank was a well-designed vehicle with a good balance of firepower, mobility, and protection. Its modular design and innovations such as the reversible periscope made it an effective vehicle for the time, despite some limitations in visibility and radio communication.

▲ Parade of Vickers tanks of the first type seen from the rear, in both single and double turret versions. Polish Archive.

VERSIONS OF THE VEHICLE

LATEST UPDATES ON 7TP

In 1938 work began to develop a new, updated version, named 9TP, with the aim of modernising the existing design. Two variants were planned: the first equipped with a 40 mm (1.57 inch) Bofors gun and the second with a more powerful gun, the choice of which, however, remained uncertain. The 9TP was equipped with a Saurer CT1D/PZLInż.155 diesel engine, instead of the 6-cylinder VBLDb diesel. The new wagon appeared with improved suspension and wider track widths. Although they were never used in combat, it is believed that at least 11 9TPs were delivered in the summer of 1939. Plans also included attempts to mount a twin 20 mm (0.79 inch) FK-A wz.38 L/73.5 gun on a 7TP tank, but no prototype was ever completed. The main limitation of the 7TP was its lack of adaptability for effective modernisation, as the original design dated back more than ten years before the outbreak of war.

At that time, Poland also sought to enter the market. Export opportunities to several countries were also evaluated, including Estonia (4 units in 1937, but the agreement was canceled), Turkey (in 1938, with a licensing agreement that was never finalized due to the outcome of disastrousthe war), Yugoslavia and Greece (a total of 36 units).

Despite its limitations, the chassis of the 7TP still proved its worth, a sign that Vickers had devised ujh good vehicle. It was considered versatile enough to create a series of even non-combat vehicles. Two prototypes, the S6R and S6T, were made in 1933. The former was equipped with an engine and front-wheel drive, while both models mounted a 115-hp PZlnż.235 diesel engine.

The turret was replaced by an armored cabin for the driver and a mechanic.

For mass production of the new artillery tractor, because that what was it was, the S6R was selected, which was modified and renamed the S7R (*Ciagnik Siedmiotonowy* Polski - Polish 7-ton truck). Before September 1939, 151 of the 350 tractors ordered were delivered, used mainly for towing 220 mm (8.66 in.) Skoda mortars. In addition, 18 S7Rs were assigned to the 10th Cavalry Brigade for transporting tanks and tankettes on special platforms. The above vehicles captured by enemy forces then remained in Wehrmacht service until the end of 1941.

▲ 7TP tank platoon with Bofors 37 mm gun during the exercise. Polish Archive.

7TP LIGHT TANK WITH DOUBLE TURRET, POLAND 1938

▲ Polish light tank DW 7TP (with double turret) of the 3rd Armoured Battalion, Cieszyn, Poland, October 1938.

VICKERS' VARIANTS A AND B

1st Variant - Tank with two 7.92 mm TMG machine guns wz. 25

All Vickers-Armstrong Ltd. tanks were delivered in the double turret (Type A) version, without initial armament as requested by the Polish General Staff. Once they arrived at their destination in Poland, they were equipped in early 1933 with two machine guns 7.92 mm wz.25 air-cooled mounted on newly developed universal spherical mounts. Hotchkiss

However, plans had long been made to arm the tanks with more reliable, water-cooled 7.92 mm wz.30 machine guns and to equip 14 tanks with a mixed armament, with a machine gun 13.2 mm wz.30 in the left turret. Nevertheless, all turrets were always equipped with squared covers for 13.2 mm magazines, even when it would not have been necessary because of the various weapon versions. The right turret, reserved for the commander, was the only one with small sleeves for signal flags. (See profiles on pages 8 and 10)Hotchkiss

2st Variant - Tank armed with 37 mm SA gun and 7.92 mm machine gun

To increase firepower, some tanks were equipped with a gun37-mm , mounted in the same universal mount, while the second turret retained the machine gun.Puteaux 7.92-mm wz.25 Initially, the guns were mounted in the left turret, only to be moved to the right turret in the fall of 1933. There are also reports of a tank Hotchkiss equipped with as many as two 37 mm cannons!

However, the 37-mm SA gun proved to be ineffective against enemy armor, determining to consider it an interim solution pending a new, more suitable weapon system. On November 9, 1932, the Chief of Staff decided to convert 22 tanks to single turret versions, using British B-type truncated cone turrets with 47 mm guns (see profiles on pages 12 and 17).

▲ The Polish Vickers tank, in its initial double turret configuration, was equipped with two 7.92 mm Hotchkiss wz.25 model machine guns. This version featured four-colour camouflage, typical of the period.

▲ A 7TP-dw - with double turret of the old type, still with the square magazines mounted on the front.

In May 1933, before the delivery of the new turrets, it was decided to temporarily arm them:
- 6 tanks with cannon 37 mm SA and 7.92 mm wz.30 machine gun,Puteaux
- 16 tanks with machine gun machine gun,Hotchkiss wz.30 13.2 mm and wz.30 7.92 mm
- 16 tanks with two 7.92 mm wz.30 machine guns.

This plan thus excluded the old wz.25 machine guns, which nevertheless remained in use for some time. Replacing the wz.25 with the wz.30 took longer than expected, and in November 1934 some tanks prepared for 37 mm guns were still equipped with the old machine guns.

Vickers double-turret tanks could also be armed with a 37-mm SA gun in the right turret and a 7.92-mm TMG wz.25 machine gun in the left turret.

3rd Variant - Tank with mixed system: 13.2 mm and 7.92 mm machine gun

In 1933, 16 tanks were rearmed with a Hotchkiss wz.30 13.2 mm machine gun in the right turret, classified as a 'heavy machine gun'. The machine guns were delivered from France in January 1933. According to plans, these tanks were to carry up to 720 13.2 mm and 2,500 7.92 mm rounds. Initially, the other turret could be armed with a wz.25. By August 1935, all double turret tanks were listed as being armed with 13.2 mm and 7.92 mm wz.30 machine guns, although this configuration is rarely documented photographically (see profiles on pages 14 and 16).

4th Variant IV - Tank with 47 mm cannon and 7.92 mm machine gun

To further improve combat capabilities, 22 single Type B turrets, armed with 47 mm Vickers QF guns, were purchased in Britain and delivered in March 1934. These turrets were equipped with 7.92 mm wz.30 machine guns, mounted to the right of the gun in a different armored cover than the standard Vickers

▲ The new Saurer VBLDd diesel engine mounted on Polish 7TP wagons.

cover. Between mid-1934 and March 1935, 22 tanks were rebuilt with these single turrets and new top plates. Each tank could carry up to 50 rounds for the cannon.

5th Variant - Tank with two 7.92 mm wz.30 machine guns

Because of the decision to retire the 13.2 mm machine guns, all remaining twin-turret tanks were rearmed with two 7.92 mm wz.30 machine guns by 1937. This was the final configuration of the twin-turret Vickers tanks used in combat in 1939. The 13.2 mm machine guns were transferred to the Navy for antiaircraft use.

■ THE C7P ARTILLERY TRACTOR

The C7P, an acronym for "*Ciągnik Siedmiotonowy Polski*" (Italian for "Polish 7-ton tractor"), was an artillery tractor employed by mechanized units of the Polish Army during the early stages of World War II. Derived for part of its hull entirely from the 7TP light tank, the C7P played a significant, if brief, role in the military operations of the time.

The arrival of the British tank in the Polish armamentarium suggested, among other things, the need for a specialized vehicle for mechanizing artillery and recovering damaged tanks. PZI (Państwowe Zakłady Inżynieryjne), Poland's main armament factory, began developing a design based on the Vickers chassis, which had meanwhile been modified and renamed to 7TP.

In 1933, the first prototype of the C7P was completed, and after a series of tests it was approved for mass production. Production began in 1935 and ended in September 1939, with about 150 built. Most of these vehicles were assigned to the 1st Heavy Artillery Regiment, where they were used to tow Škoda heavy mortars wz. 32 220 mm, each of which required as many as three C7Ps for transport. Eighteen units were

▲ The picture shows the rear of the Polish 7TP light tank, with a view of the muffler perforated for air intakes.

C7P ARTILLERY TRACTOR, POLAND 1939

▲ Artillery tractor belonging to an unidentified unit. Poland, September 1939.

7TP LIGHT TANK WITH DOUBLE TURRET, POLAND 1939

▲ 7TP light tank (double turret) belonging to the 2nd Light Tank Company of the Warsaw Defence Command, Warsaw, Poland, September 1939.

▲▼► Three pictures of the Polish artillery tractor de-named C7P, pictured above pulling a Skoda heavy howitzer.

Left and below: two pictures of the tractor, which ended up in the hands of the German armed forces after the brief and catastrophic Polish campaign of 1939. The Germans reused most of these vehicles at least until 1941. Péter Mujzer archive.

C7P ARTILLERY TRACTOR, GERMANIC USE 1939-1941

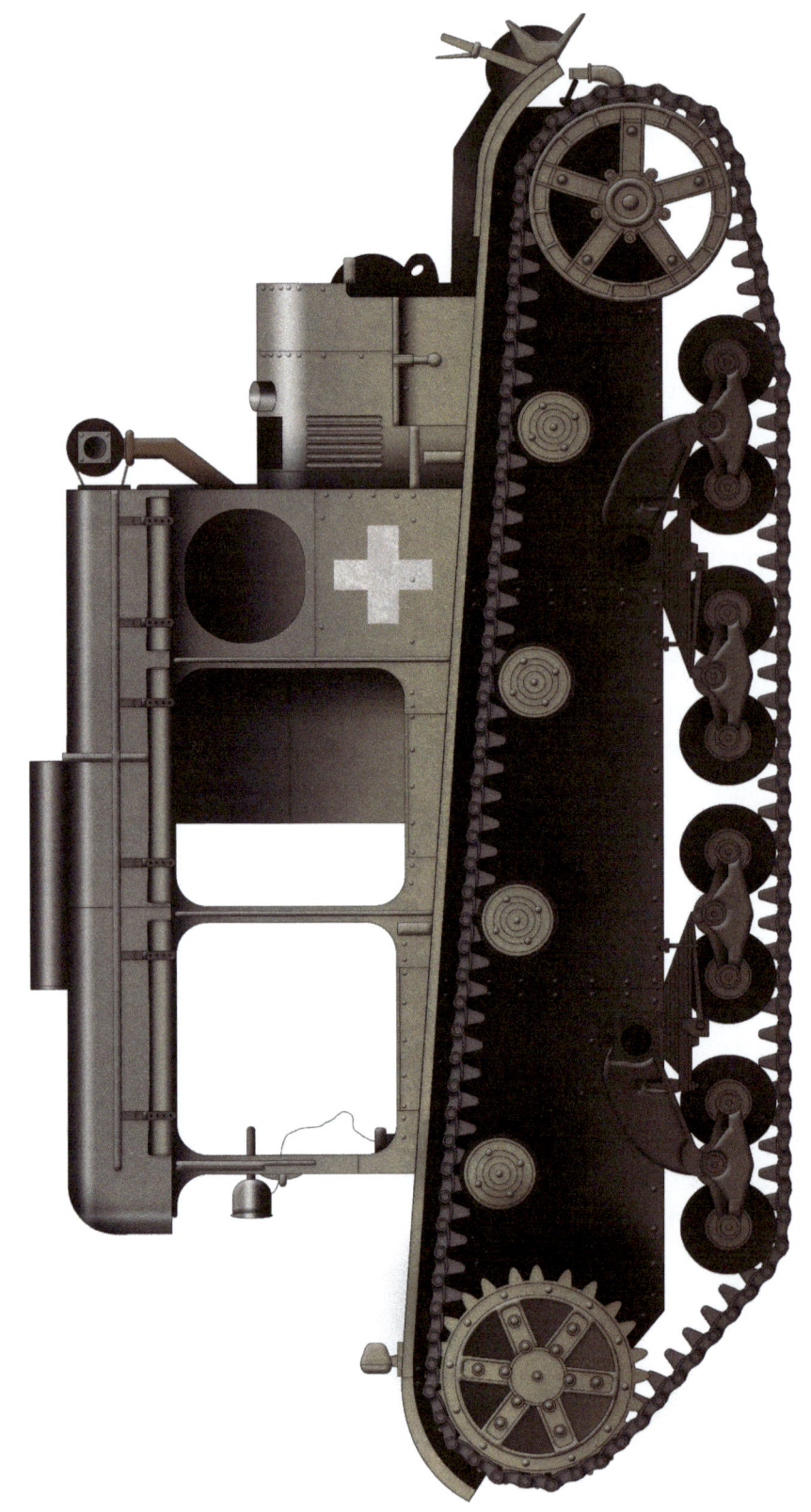

▲ Artillery tractor recovered for use by German occupation troops. Poland, 1939-1941.

instead assigned to armored formations equipped with 7TP, Vickers and Renault R35 tanks purchased from France.

However, as early as 1939, Polish commands realized that the number of available C7Ps was insufficient and ordered an additional thirty-two tractors, although it is unclear whether these were ever delivered. In addition, in the 1930s, the Polish military engineers tested two C7Ps to assess their usefulness in railroad construction and maintenance and as mobile workshops, but the project was not followed up.

Specifications

The C7P basically consisted of the hull of the 7TP tank, stripped of the turret and part of the superstructure, which were then replaced by a quadrangular cabin that housed the crew of two (commander and pilot) and up to four passengers. The chassis and rolling train remained unchanged, maintaining the same reliability and robustness as the 7TP. The rolling train consisted of eight small coupled load-bearing wheels on each side, with leaf spring suspension and rocker arms. The driving wheel was positioned at the front, while the deflection wheel, at the rear, was slightly elevated.

The armored hull, except for the removed parts, did not undergo significant modifications. The engine, was the usual Saurer diesel six-cylinder 115 hp, and was located in the rear compartment and obviously diesel-powered.

Weighing about 8.5 tons, the C7P reached a maximum speed of 26 km/h and a range of 150 km. For recovery missions, the tractor was equipped with a winch and a hitch pin, with a maximum load capacity of 5,000 kg.

In fact, the C7P represented an innovative attempt to adapt a light tank to a logistical and support role, demonstrating the ingenuity of Polish military industry in the 1930s. However, its use was limited by the outbreak of World War II and the rapid invasion of Poland by German forces. Despite its short operational career, the C7P remains an interesting example of a Polish military vehicle of the period, bearing witness to a crucial period in European history.

▲ A C7P tractor belonging to the 10th Polish mechanised cavalry brigade in 1939.

▲ A 7TP tank with two turrets is loaded onto a rail car for fast transport during training or military operations.

▼ Polish military vehicles parade in front of national authorities and representatives of senior French and British Allied officers. In the foreground a 155 gun pulled by a C7P tractor.

▲ 7TP tank seen from above.

OTHER DERIVATIVES

The 7TP tank derivative series requires the reporting of at least three vehicles. The radio command tank, the tankbulldozer, and finally plans were made to develop an anti-aircraft self-propelled vehicle by installing on the tank, again deprived of turret and superstructure, two 20-mm FK-A wz. 38 L/73.5 automatics, but in 1938 all resources were reserved for the expansion of armored forces, and this project also lapsed.

The radio control tank

Polish Vickers tanks customarily lacked radios, using colored flags for communications, as did most tanks of the time. In 1937-1938, one tank from the Armored Weapons Training Center was experimentally modified with an RKB/C radio, which required shielding of the wiring. Plans were made to upgrade eight other single turret tanks, but the plans were abandoned for lack of radios. It is unclear how many Vickers were actually equipped with radios, but there is only one photo of a double turret tank with radio (see p. 7 and profile on p. 16).

According to other sources, just before the war, four tanks of the 12th Company received RKB/C (discontinued) radios. Some authors speculate that three had only receivers, but without evidence. It is uncertain whether four tanks of the 121st Company also had radios.

The mounted experimental radio was in the hull, equipped with a 3.5 m bamboo antenna. On double-turret tanks, the antenna was carried horizontally between the turrets when not in use.

Bulldozer tank

The conversion of some vehicles equipped with a front bulldozer is also known. It was attached to the hull by means of jointed arms and a maneuvering system operated within the tank that was of the two-turret type (see related profile in the book).

▲ Three models of the Polish 7TP tank: one with the two turrets, one with the classic single turret of the Polish type, and finally, at the bottom, the version made for the engineer with the bulldozer attached to the front of the tank.

MILITARY ENGINEER TANK, POLAND 1939

▲ Light 7TP tank equipped as a bulldozer tank with a bulldozer attached to the front of the vehicle. Poland 1939.

▲ 7TP tank front and rear view.

▲▼ The occupation of Silesia by Czeski Cieszyn el 1938 resulted in a semi-triumphal military parade of Polish tank columns and soldiers. In the towns, flowers flew on the tanks, the Polish majority in the region welcomed them as liberators. Very soon, however, not a few regretted this, and almost 20 per cent of the population abandoned the region within the first few months. The occupation lasted only 11 months.

SINGLE TURRET 7TP LIGHT TANK, POLAND 1939

▲ 7TP light tank - Tank with 'chequered' camouflage, 2nd Light Tank Battalion, Łódź Army, Battle of Włodawa, Poland, 15 September 1939.

OPERATIONAL USE

■ PRE-WAR OPERATIONAL SERVICE

Due to the very short endurance of the Polish army following the aggressive and disruptive invasion of German armored troops, the operational life of the Polish tanks was summed up in only two episodes. Those prior to the outbreak of World War II, such as the occupation of Polish-majority regions residing in Czechoslovakia as a result of the Munich Accords of 1938. And precisely those engaged in the bloody conflict against Hitler's troops that resulted in a rapid collapse of Polish forces. Any further use of Polish tanks and vehicles after that date was German use of them, especially in Russia.

The occupation of Zaolzia

The first Vickers tanks delivered to Poland formed the V fast tank company of the 3rd Armoured Regiment in Warsaw, distinguishing it from the slower Renault FT from the outset. After a reorganisation in February 1934, the unit became the 3rd Armoured Battalion (Batalion Pancerny) in Warsaw.

In that year, only nine tanks were operational: six in the combat company and three in the training company. With the arrival of the new 7TP tanks in 1937, the Vickers were transferred to the 2nd Armoured Battalion in Żurawica, near Przemyśl. Another unit equipped with Vickers from 1934 was the experimental (11th) Armoured Battalion at the Armoured Weapons Training Centre (CWBrPanc) in Modlin.

These tanks were mainly used for training, manoeuvres and assigned to the 10th Cavalry Brigade, the only experimental motorised brigade. Between 4 and 20 September 1938, 23 Vickers tanks from both battalions took part in large-scale manoeuvres in Volinia, a region east of Poland now in the Ukraine, forming a company assigned to the 10th Motorised Cavalry Brigade (10.BK). The purpose of these exercises was to prepare for action to recapture Zaolzie, a Polish-majority province annexed by Czechoslovakia in 1918. Taking advantage of the Czechoslovak crisis after the Munich Agreement, Poland occupied Zaolzie without a fight on 22 September 1938, with the 10.BK assigned to Operation Group 'Śląsk' (Silesia).

The brigade and its tanks remained in the region for two months, basically participating in parades for the benefit of the Polish majority living in the region. At the end of November, two Vickers platoons

▲ Beautiful view of a two-tower Vickers tank driving through the town of Czeski Cieszyn, capital of Zeolsia.

▲▼ More pictures related to the Silesian occupation of Czeski Cieszyn in 1938. Among other things, this large collection of photographs is also the largest iconographic record of the 7TP/Vickers tanks. Polish Archive.

SINGLE TURRET 7TP LIGHT TANK, POLAND 1939

▲ Light tank 7TP - of the 1st Light Tank Battalion (Prusy Army), with the standard 'horizontal pattern', Battle of Głowaczów, 9-10 September 1939.

▲▼ More pictures of the Silesian occupation of Czeski Cieszyn in 1938. One is immediately struck by the warm welcome of the people, which Poland, however, did not manage well. Polish Archive.

joined the Operations Group 'Podhale' for the annexation of part of Spisz as well, but were not involved in fighting in Jaworzyna, remaining in the area until December. This occupation ended up having negative repercussions in the eyes of the democratic countries of the world.

In 1938, Nazi Germany after the Sudetenland also annexed Czechoslovakia. Cunningly, however, it succeeded in presenting the annexation of this very young state, born in 1918 from the ashes of the Habsburg Empire, by inviting the Czechs' other neighbours - Poles, Hungarians - to the partition banquet.

Poland then sent an ultimatum to Czechoslovakia, demanding the withdrawal of troops and police Prague already on its knees bowed down, and the Polish army, led by General Władysław Bortnowski, annexed an area of about 800 km² with 228,000 inhabitants. Germany gave up a small province in exchange for propaganda advantages. Poland was accused of complicity with the Nazi regime, damaging its international reputation.

The Polish population of Zaolzie enthusiastically welcomed the annexation, seeing it as a liberation, with placards such as: 'We have been waiting for you for 600 years' received by Warsaw's tanks, but this population soon changed its mind. The new Polish authorities imposed policies of strict 'polonisation': Polish became the only official language, the use of Czech and German was banned, and many Czechs and Germans were forced to emigrate. Czech institutions were dismantled, creating discontent among the locals. Almost 20% of the inhabitants of the occupation zone left the area, and Catholic churches were reorganised under Polish administration.

The annexation eventually lasted only 11 months, until the German invasion of Poland in September 1939. In July 1939, the 2nd Battalion had 20 tanks, the CWBrPanc had 17 and one last tank was in use at the Technical Office for Armoured Weapons. In each battalion, five tanks were mobilisation reserve (class A), 12 were for mobilisation and training (class B), and three in the 2nd Battalion were for training only (class C). Due to the intensive use for training, many tanks were worn out by 1939.

▲▼ More pictures of the Silesian occupation of Czeski Cieszyn in 1938. Less than a year later this ended up under Nazi occupation. Polish Archive.

THE CAMPAIGN OF SEPTEMBER 1919

As thick clouds loomed over the nation during the general mobilization of August 1939. On paper the confrontation immediately appeared improbable for Polish forces; while Warsaw counted armored forces in companies, the Germans reasoned in divisions. What about the Polish armored forces then? Vickers/7TP tanks were assigned to two light tank companies belonging to the only two motorized brigades in the Polish Army.

The wartime events of the 121st Light Tank Company

The 121st Light Tank Company was formed in Modlin from the 11th Armored Battalion to support the 10th Cavalry Brigade, while the 2nd Armored Battalion, stationed in Żurawica, formed the 12th Light Tank Company for the Warsaw Armored-Motorized Brigade (WBP-M).

Each company was equipped with 16 tanks, including 10-11 with a single turret and 5-6 with double turrets. The unit was organized into a command squad, which included the commander's tank, and three operational platoons, each consisting of five tanks. It is likely that in 1939 the platoons were equipped with a combination of three single-turret and two double-turret vehicles.

There is some uncertainty about the actual number of tanks in the 121st Company. There was talk, however, for it to appear clear of ridiculous numbers compared to those available to the Nazis. The 10th Cavalry Brigade, complained that the unit had only 7-8 tanks, some spoke of 9 and you will understand very little changes... However, according to official data, the company should have been fully equipped with all 16 tanks. It is assumed, however, that it had at least a dozen vehicles, since a smaller number would be inconsistent with the losses incurred in the last clashes in which the unit was involved.

The 121st Light Tank Company, operated in support of the 10th Cavalry Brigade (10. BK). Its main mission was to flank Polish motorized cavalry in containment and slowdown operations against two German armored divisions in the mountains south of Poland, beginning September 1, 1939.

Given the limited availability of armored units, the 121st Company was initially kept in reserve. Later, to-

▲ Polish armoured column in great splendour shortly before the tragedy. Polish Archive.

gether with two companiestankette , it was employed as a kind of "rapid intervention force," intervening at the most critical points on the front to counter enemy advances.

On September 3, 1939, the company's tanks took part in a counterattack along the roadKrzeczów-Skomielna , twice succeeding in pushing back the infantry troops of the German 2nd Armored Division, which threatened the flank of the 10th Mounted Rifle Regiment.

On the following day, 4 September, the tanks of the 121st again supported the 24th Lancer Regiment's attack on the village of Kasina Wielka, operating in collaboration with the 101st Reconnaissance Tank Company. During the clash, they helped to stop the advance of units of the German 4th Light Division and 3rd Mountain Division. On that day, the German forces suffered the loss of three tanks and two armoured cars. The Polish resistance managed to halt the enemy advance, albeit at the cost of two Vickers tanks and some tankettes. In the following days, the company continued to fight with intensity, suffering further losses. On 6 September, during a battle in the village of Trzciana, near Wiśnicz, another tank was destroyed.

On September 8, during a night retreat, the company's tanks, positioned in the rear, ran out of fuel near the village of Przyłęk, east of Mielec. This episode resulted in the loss of the only operational tanks of the 10th Armored Battalion (10.BK).

However, the company managed to find some makeshift fuel in the surrounding villages, but the amount was not enough for all the vehicles. Only three tanks managed to reach Kolbuszowa on the evening of 8 September. Later, the command of the Krakow Army Armoured Forces ordered them to move to Nisko, across the San River, where they were assigned to the 6th Infantry Division to boost troop morale. On 13 September, they were again transferred to the 21st Mountain Division, part of the 'Boruta' operational group. On 15 September, they participated in the Battle of Oleszyce against the German 45th Infantry Division. Unfortunately, on 16 September, the 21st Division, surrounded, was forced to surrender. During the fighting, one tank was destroyed by artillery near Koziejówka, while the other two fell into German hands. The rest of the 121st Company reached Kolbuszowa on 9 September, where it was engaged in the defence of the town against the German 2nd Panzer Division. The fighting, which lasted throughout the afternoon and evening, resulted in significant losses on both sides. The Polish company lost three vehicles while covering the retreat of the Polish troops towards the river Łęg. Despite the losses, the unit

▲ Evocative image that refers to the hardships of a brutally invaded nation. Polish Archive.

continued to fight alongside the 6th Infantry Division 'Boruta'. According to some reports, six tanks took part in further fighting, particularly during the crossing of the Tanew River and the attacks on Narol and Bełżec between 17 and 18 September. By that point, however, the company had been reduced to three tanks and about twenty men, but their fighting spirit remained intact and they ceased to exist as a force capable of opposing the German armoured forces.

The wartime fortunes of the 12th Light Tank Company

The second Polish armored unit to employ Vickers tanks was the 12th Light Tank Company of the Warsaw Armored Motorized Brigade (WBP-M), led by Captain Czesław Blok, a determined officer but aware of the limitations of his equipment. During mobilization, only four of their tanks-those of the company commander and platoon commanders-were equipped with radio devices, a rare luxury for Polish forces at the time. These devices, however, proved more a symbol of hope than an effective tool, given the confusion and chaos that would characterize the days ahead.

August and the first weeks of September 1939 were spent in frantic training along the right bank of the Vistula. Vickers engines roared in the summer heat as sweaty, anxious crews practiced maneuvers they knew were little more than a pale reflection of the firepower and coordination of German forces. The Brigade was aware that it was an island of modernity in a sea of antiquated equipment and tactics, but even the Vickers, while advanced by Polish standards, were already obsolete compared to German Panzers.

On September 13, the 12th Company went into action for the first time, against the German bridgehead on the Vistula near Annopol. The attack, however, turned into a disaster. Without infantry support, the Polish tanks advanced too quickly, exposing themselves to concentrated fire from the German 4th Light Division's anti-tank guns. Two Vickers were reduced to smoking wreckage, while the others, retreating, were mistaken for enemies by Polish infantry and machine-gunned. Only a few crew members managed to save themselves, wounded and shocked.

▲ A Polish crew around its two-turret 7TP during September 1939. Polish Archive.

SINGLE TURRET 7TP LIGHT TANK, POLAND 1939

▲ Light tank 7TP - of the 2ⁿᵈ Light Tank Battalion, Poland, September 1939.

In the following days, the situation worsened. The tanks, already worn out from intensive use, began to fail. Six Vickers had to be abandoned along the muddy roads of eastern Poland as fuel shortages became an increasingly pressing problem. The exhausted crews fought not only against the Germans, but also against disastrous logistics and lack of supplies.

On September 17, as the Soviet Union, joining the Germans, invaded Poland from the east, two surviving Vickers were engaged in a clash with two German armored cars near Krasnobród. The Vickers' guns fired, destroying the enemy vehicles in a brief but intense exchange of fire. It was a small victory, a ray of light in an increasingly dark landscape.

But the Brigade's fate was sealed. The Battle of Tomaszów Lubelski, fought between September 18 and 20, was the last, desperate attempt to break through to Lviv. The eight remaining Vickers, along with a handful of tankettes and 7TP tanks, supported Polish infantry assaults against German positions. The fighting was furious: Polish tanks advanced under enemy fire, their 47mm guns trying to break through enemy lines. But the German Panzers and anti-tank guns were too numerous. One after another, the Vickers were hit and destroyed. At dawn on September 20, only a lone 7TP was still operational. The Brigade, now reduced to a shadow of its former self, was forced to surrender.

The remaining Vickers tanks, those not assigned to 12th Company, followed an equally tragic fate. Gathered in the 3rd Armored Weapons Reserve Center (OZ 3), some of them were destroyed by Soviet tanks during the invasion from the east. Others, abandoned due to mechanical failure or lack of fuel, fell into German or Soviet hands. None of these vehicles were ever reused by the victors: the Germans considered them obsolete, while the Soviets studied them briefly before relegating them to history.

▲ After only thirty-six days of unprecedented resistance, the Polish armed forces had to capitulate. Polish Archive.

SINGLE TURRET 7TP LIGHT TANK, POLAND 1939

▲ Light tank 7TP - of the 3rd Light Tank Battalion, Poland, September 1939.

POLISH 7TP LIGHT TANK

▲▼ These two images are particularly significant of the Polish tragedy. Above: 7TP tanks of the Polish army parade proudly in front of the national authorities in Warsaw. Below: same place, again in the Polish capital, but this time parading are the 7TP tanks to which the German occupiers applied their symbols, in order to re-employ them (until 1941) in their armed forces. Polish Archive.

POLISH 7TP LIGHT TANK   TWE | 53

SINGLE TURRET 7TP LIGHT TANK, POLAND 1939

▲ 7TP light tank - single turret, 2nd Light Tank Company, operating in the Wola sector, Poland, 13 September 1939.

CAMOUFLAGE AND MARKINGS

■ INITIAL MIMETICS

Between 1932 and 1936, Polish armored vehicles used an early camouflage scheme, commonly called: "Japanese camouflage" in Poland. Its normative source has so far not been found in the archives; therefore, there are some doubts about the colors used. According to the latest research, based on the examination of museum objects, it consisted of large irregular patches of yellowish sand, olive green and light blue-gray, separated by thin black stripes; blue-gray was the lightest shade. Traditional publications commonly cited the color dark brown instead of blue-gray and considered sand the lightest shade. Initially there was a standard stain pattern, but many tanks had different patterns or had some colors reversed. The interior was blue-gray, the inner surfaces of the hatches were camouflaged.
Before the introduction of "Japanese" camouflage, five "iron" TK-3s of the first series were experimentally painted with black and white spots, five with blue-gray spots and five with yellow and green spots.

■ LATE MIMETICS

Since 1936 a new standard three-colour camouflage scheme was introduced for all Polish military vehicles. It consisted of irregular patches of greyish sand and dark brown (sepia) airbrushed onto an olive green base colour. The patches had smooth transitions, their shape was mainly horizontal, often almost rectangular or rhomboid. There was no standard patch pattern, although the patterns used were similar (the instructions only gave examples of views of the front and right side of the TKS). The patches often created a kind of chessboard, especially on the late series vehicles. Transitions between colours are often not very evident in black and white photos. The interiors were painted sand, including the hatches. Almost all tankettes were repainted with the new camouflage in the late 1930s, only a few tankettes used as armoured train draisins and perhaps some training vehicles remained with the old camouflage in September 1939.

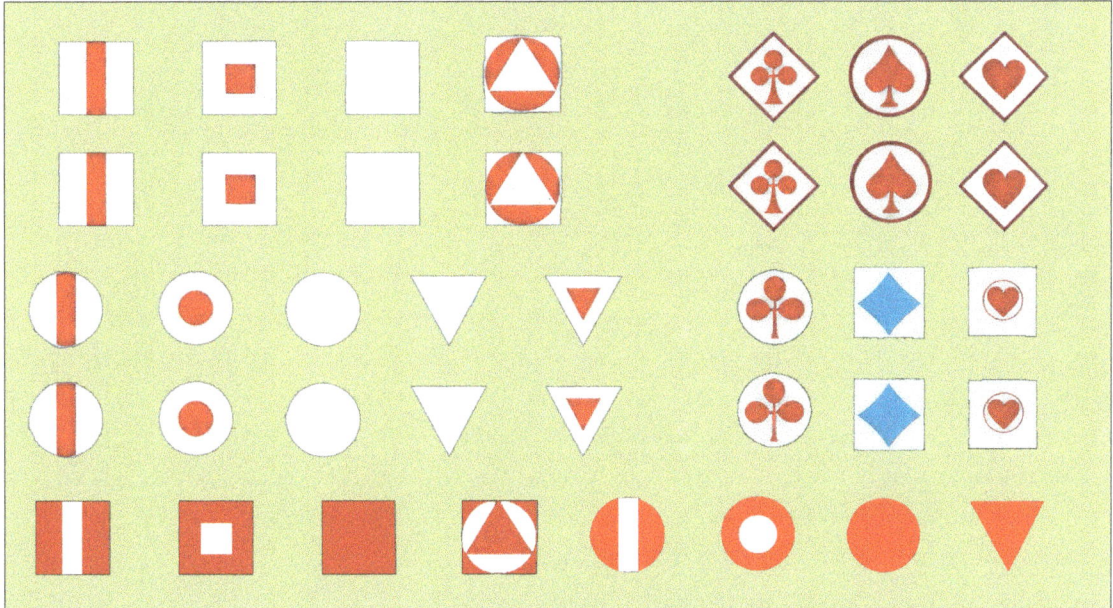

▲ Various distinguishing marks of Polish tanks. Like the French, the Poles also adopted card suits.

■ DISTINCTIVE SYMBOLS

From the early 1930s until 1939, Polish armored vehicles bore no nationality insignia. Before the war, tactical sheet metal insignia attached for training purposes were used - discs (the 1st platoon), triangles (the 2nd) or squares (the 3rd). The insignia were white with a vertical red stripe for the platoon commander, or with a small red disk, triangle or square inside for the second-in-command. Squadron commanders had an insignia with a triangle in a circle in a square. Their colors could also be reversed.

In September 1939, tankettes generally bore no insignia. The use of any insignia was prohibited in case of war by the 1938 regulations, however, several photos are known of tankettes captured in September 1939 that still bore tactical insignia. The 1939 photos also show a few instances of unofficial unit and perhaps individual insignia painted on tankettes (the Pomeranian Griffon for TK-3s of the 81st Armored Unit, arrows for TK-3s of an unknown unit, the rocking horse-perhaps on a tank of the 10th Cavalry Brigade, and a photo of a hand armed with a sword on the TK-3). The four-digit registration numbers were painted only on the front plates until 1936, then the plates with the new numbers were brought back inside.

▲ Polish military vehicles, including several 7TPs with Vickers guns in camouflage outfits.

OTHER USERS

In addition to Poland, obviously main user the bandtankinterested, some countries such as Estonia and some countriesBalkan ; however, the precipitation of events nipped any such market in the bud.

• **Countries involved**: around 1938 At that time, Poland also tried to enter the market by offering its versions of the 7TP light tank. A number of export opportunities to various countries were then pursued and evaluated, including Estonia (4 units in 1937, but the agreement was canceled), Turkey (in 1938, with a licensing agreement that was never finalized due to the outcome of disastrousthe war), Yugoslavia and Greece (a total of 36 units).

• **Germany**: after the end of Fall Weiss (white case) i.e., the military campaign in Poland, the Third Reich captured most of the Polish military vehicles. These vehicles were initially reused sporadically between 1940 and 1941. All the vehicles and of course also the light tanks /tP and their variants, especially the artillery tractor were repainted in the standard color of armored vehicles (Panzergrau) and equipped with black and white crosses as recognition symbols. They also received the new designation of Pzkpfw 7TP (p) (where "p" stands for polnische, or Polish in German).
Light tanks especially were paraded during the victory parade held in Warsaw on October 8. Later, they would be used as police tanks or assigned to pulling artillery pieces.

• **Soviet Union**: the Soviets, who later entered the invasion of Poland captured one or a few more single-engine 7TPs and tested them between 1939 and 1940 at Kubinka; however, it seems they were not impressed and abandoned the thing.

DATA SHEET			
	Vickers A	**Vickers B**	**7TP**
Length	4,88 m	4,88 m	4,56 m
Width	2,41 m	2,41 m	2,41 m
Height	2,08 m	2,17 m	2,27 m
Weight	7,2 t	7,34 t	9,9 t
Crew	3	3	3
Engine	Armstrong-Siddeley 4-cylinder 80 hp	Armstrong-Siddeley 4-cylinder 80 hp	Saurer VGLD or VBL-Db 6-cylinder diesel
Maximum speed	37 km/h	37 km/h	37 km/h
Developed by	Vickers-Armstrong Ltd	Vickers-Armstrong Ltd	PZI su licenza
Entry into service	1932	1934	1938
Armour thickness	5-13 mm	5-13 mm	13-17 mm
Armament	2 Browning 7.92 mm WZ.30 successively	4.7 mm Vickers gun 1 Browning 7.92 mm	1 gun Bofors WZ. 36 37mm
Units	38	22	132

POLISH 7TP LIGHT TANK

7TP SINGLE TURRET LIGHT TANK, CAPTURED BY THE GERMANS 1939

▲ Single turret 7TP light tank, one of the first to be captured and immediately converted with swastikas painted on its chassis and immediately put into combat. Poland, September 1939.

PERISCOPE GUNDLACH

The Gundlach Periscope represented a revolutionary breakthrough in military technology. Designed by Polish engineer Rudolf Gundlach, this device was first introduced in Polish 7TP tanks as early as late 1935 and patented the following year under the name **Peryskop obrotowy Gundlacha** (Rotating PeriscopeGundlach). Its main innovation lay in allowing the tank commander to obtain a full 360-degree view without having to change positions. Using a dual eyepiece system, the commander could rotate the periscope and observe the area behind simply by looking through the second eyepiece, eliminating the need to physically move inside the turret. This feature was particularly useful in early tanks with narrow turrets and fixed seats, which made it difficult to use multiple periscopes or an independent rotating dome.

In the same year, the periscope Gundlach was officially adopted by the Polish Army under the name "Reversible Periscope G wz. 34". Initially employed on TKS , it later found wide use in 7TP light tanks. Shortly before the outbreak of World War II, the design was shared with the British, who integrated it into their tanks, including: tankettesCrusader, the Churchill, the Valentine, the Cromwell, and later also in the American M4 Sherman. After the German and Soviet invasion of Poland in 1939, many Polish tanks equipped with the periscope Gundlach were captured. This allowed Germany, the USSR and Romania to copy the invention and use it in turn. In particular, the Soviets adopted it under the name MK-4, and implemented it en masse in their tanks, including the famous T-34 up to the modern T-70.

The spread of the periscope Gundlach was also aided by prewar military cooperation between Poland and the United Kingdom. Indeed, the patent was sold to Vickers-Armstrong for the symbolic sum of one zloty, and the device became a standard for British tanks. After the war, this technology spread globally, remaining in use virtually unchanged for nearly 50 years until it was gradually replaced by more advanced electronic systems.

The Gundlach periscope was not only a technical innovation, but a symbol of Polish ingenuity that, despite tragic wartime events, managed to leave a lasting imprint on the history of military technology.

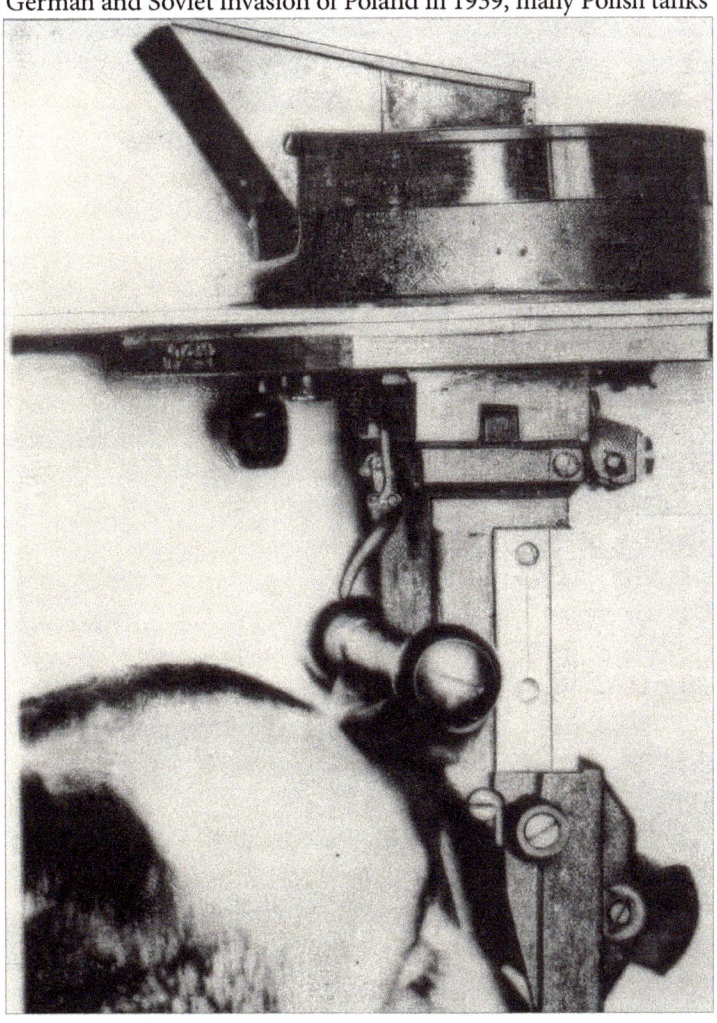

▲ The Gundlach periscope, an interesting Polish invention.

7TP SINGLE TURRET LIGHT TANK, CAPTURED BY THE GERMANS 1940

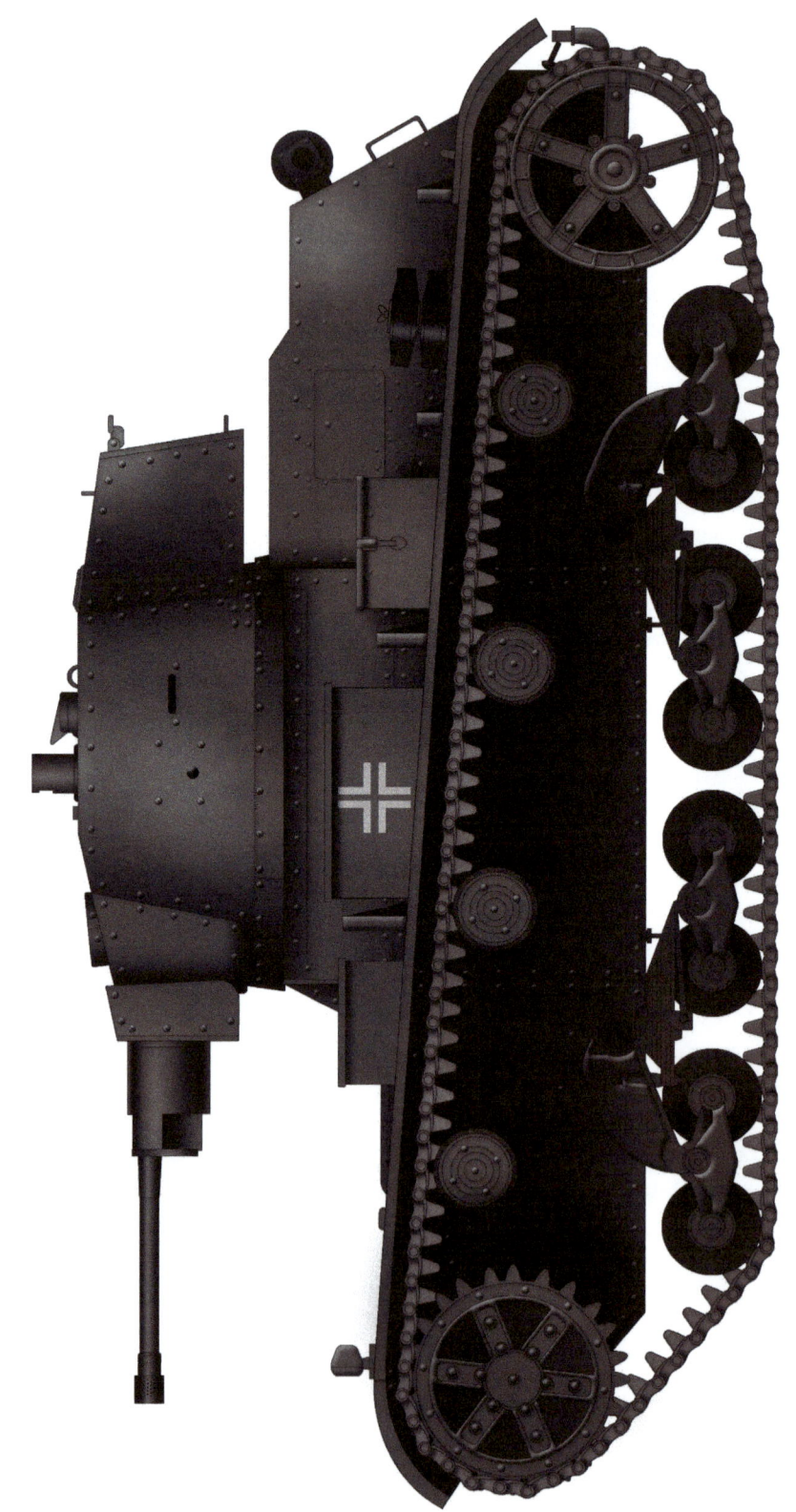

▲ 7TP light tank for German use renamed as Pzkpfw 731(p), which served in France in May-June 1940, and subsequently in Norway. Others were sent for police and anti-partisan warfare in occupied territories in Belarus and Ukraine

▲ Military review of the Polish General Staff to an armoured 7TP light tank formation.
▼ Two pictures of Polish 7TP single turret tanks captured and observed by German troops.

POLISH 7TP LIGHT TANK

7TP DOUBLE TURRET LIGHT TANK CAPTURED BY THE GERMANS, POLAND 1940

▲ Light tank 7TP – double turret for German use as PzKpfw 7TP(p) police unit, Polish General Government, spring 1940.

▲ German soldiers inspect an abandoned Vickers Type B from the 121st Light Tank Company discovered in Kasina Wielka, southern Poland.

▼ Polish 7TP tank captured by the Germans and exhibited at the Leipzig Fair in 1940 for the German public. The gun barrel of the tank appears to have no muzzle brake. Bundesarchiv.

SINGLE TURRET 7TP LIGHT TANK, GERMAN USE 1942

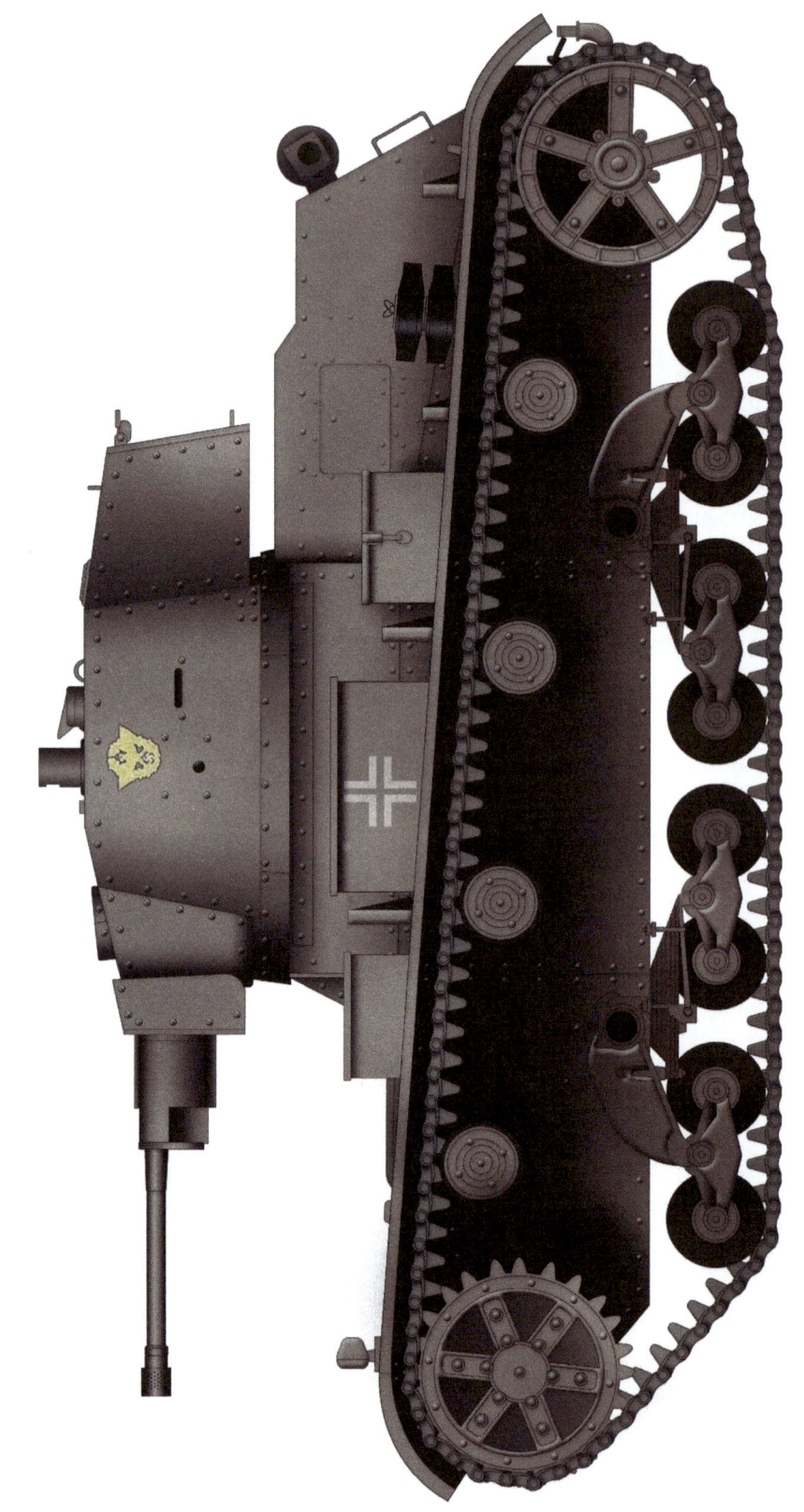

▲ 7TP light tank - single turret, of the Polizei Panzer Kompanie 'Ost' Belarus, summer 1942.

POLISH 7TP LIGHT TANK

▲ German soldiers observe two newly captured 7TP tanks. Archive photo Péter Mujzer.

▼ A 7TP tank formerly used by the Germans and then abandoned in flaws. Archive photo Péter Mujzer.

SINGLE TURRET 7TP LIGHT TANK, GERMAN USE 1943

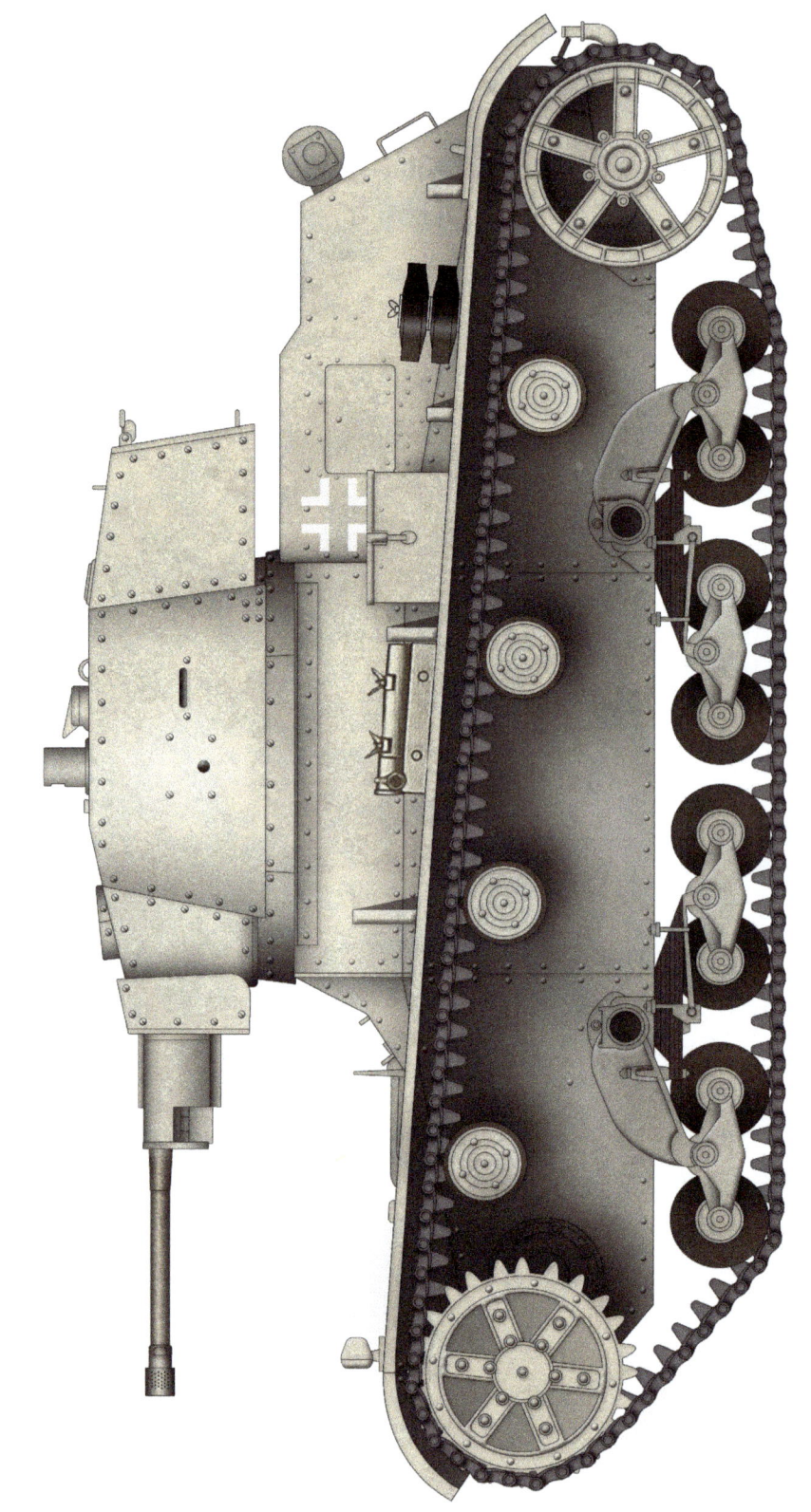

▲ 7TP light tank - single turret, German renamed as Pzkpfw Polizei Panzer Kompanie 'ost', Russia 1943.

▲ Two single turret 7TP tanks put out of action in September 1939 during Operation Fall Weiss.
▼ Polish 7TP single turret tanks captured and observed by German troops.

SINGLE TURRET 7TP LIGHT TANK, GERMAN USE 1943

▲ 7TP light tank – single turret, German renamed as Pzkpfw Polizei Panzer Kompanie 'ost', Eastern Front 1943.

POLISH 7TP LIGHT TANK

▲ The 7TP was not a 'Beutepanzer' particularly used by the Germans. It was recovered in several dozen units in 1939 and reused by them for reconnaissance, police and mostly as an artillery tractor with the C7V variant.

BIBLIOGRAPHY

- Barbarski, Krzysztof: *armi corazzate polacche 1939-45*. Londra, Osprey Publications, Vanguard 30, 1982.
- David R. Higgins: *Panzer contro 7TP, Polonia 1939*. Oxford, Osprey Publishing, 2015.
- Jonac, Adam: *Pojazdy Mechaniczne Wojska Polskiego 1939*. Warsawa, ZP Grupa, 2010.
- Jonac. - Szubanski R. - Tarczynski J.: *Pojazdy Wojska Polskiego 1939*. Varsavia, WKL, 1990.
- Magnuski, Janusz: *Czolg Rozpoznawczy TK(TKS)*. Varsavia, MON, 1975.
- Magnuski, *"Czołg lekki 7TP" vol.I,* Militaria, 1996;
- Janusz Magnuski, *"7TP vol.II",* Militaria (317), Warsaw 2009.
- L. Komuda, *"Polski czołg lekki 7TP",* TBiU nr 21, 1973;
- A. Jońca, R. Szubański, J. Tarczyński, *"Pojazdy Wojska Polskiego 1939",* WKŁ, 1990;
- J. Magnuski, *"Produkcja czołgów 7TP 1935-39 r.",* nTW 12/1996;
- J. Magnuski, *"Angielski lekki czołg Vickers Mark E w polskiej służbie",* nTW 5/1999;
- R. Szubański, *"Polska broń pancerna 1939",* wydawnictwo MON, 1982;
- Nigel Thomas: *Hitler's Blitzkrieg Enemies 1940*, Oxford, Osprey Publication, 2014.
- Prenat, Jamie: *Polish Armor of the Blitzkrieg*, Oxford, Osprey Publications, New Vanguard 224, 2015.
- Surhone Lambert: *TKS: Tankette, Carden Loyd tankette, Invasion of Poland, Machine Gun, Panzer I, Panzer 35(t), Polish Army Museum, Kubinka Tank Museum*
- S. J. Zaloga- Madej, Victor: *The Polish Campaign 1939*, New York, Hippocrene Books, 1991.
- S. J. Zaloga (2003) Poland 1939 *The birth of Blitzkrieg,* Osprey Publishing
- Walter J. Spielberger, Hilary Louis Doyle: *Beute-Kfz und Panzer der Wehrmacht* – Motorbuch Verlag,
- Paweł Rozdżestwieński: *Czołg Lekki 7TP. In: Wielki Leksykon Uzbrojenia Wrzesień 1939*. Band 1. Edipresse Polska, Warschau 2012,
- Jędrzej Korbal: *Czołg 7TP i wyposażenie cz.1. In: Wielki Leksykon Uzbrojenia Wydanie Specjalne*. Band 6. Edipresse Polska, Warschau 2019, I
- Jędrzej Korbal: *Czołg 7TP i wyposażenie cz.2. In: Wielki Leksykon Uzbrojenia Wydanie Specjalne*. Band 7. Edipresse Polska, Warschau 2019.
- R. Szubański, „*Polska broń pancerna 1939*", wydawnictwo MON, 1982.
- Wielki Leksykon *Uzbrojenia Wrzesień 1939 Tom 1*. Czołg lekki 7TP
- Waldemar Trojca - *Polski Wrzesień 1939 Foto album*. Trojca Katowice 2002
- J. Ledwoch (2009) *Vickers 6-ton E/F,* Militaria
- J. Ledwoch (2009) *Vickers 6-ton E,* Militaria
- B. T. White, *British Tanks 1915-1945,* Ian Allan LTD.
- D. H. Higgins (2015) *Panzer II vs. 7TP,* Osprey Publishing
- T. A. Bartyzel and A. Kaminski (1996) *Polish Army Vehicles 1939-1945,* Intech 2.
- C. Czolg, *Armor in Panzerne Profile 1,* PELTA.

PUBLISHED TITLES

TWE-036 EN

www.ingramcontent.com/pod-product-compliance
Lightning Source LLC
LaVergne TN
LVHW072120060526
838201LV00068B/4928